7 Keys To Changing Any Attitude
Or Circumstance In Your Life

by Linda McNeil   2/2/98

Best wishes to Linda from Linda McNeil

Open Mind Publishing

First Edition
First Printing October, 1997
Manufactured in the United States of America

Library of Congress Catalog Card Number: 97-92702.
ISBN 1-891446-00-2

Open Mind Publishing
Golden, CO

ACKNOWLEDGEMENTS:

Thank you, Maureen Christensen, for: your reading time, constant encouragement, never doubting, always supporting, unconditional love, and for teaching me about me.

Thank you, Cia Wenzel, for: being one of the most positive people I know, your reading time, watching my finances, scuba diving, and always believing in me.

Thank you, Barbara Knapp-Colston, for: being a best friend since the 4th grade and always being there for me in love and companionship.

Thank you, Paul Williams, for: your very generous contributions to this book and for being a friend and reader.

Thank you, Bob Hanna, for: coming into my life at such an exciting time, your friendship, generosity, constancy, cards, calls and amazing sense of humor.

Thank you, Mom and Dad, for: providing me a loving childhood and teaching me a deep appreciation of nature and the out-of-doors. You also taught me how to work hard—I've needed that!

Thank you, Deborah Hubbel, for: friendship, your service story, sharing your darling daughter, Melissa, to teach me more about the joys of play.

Thank you, Charol Messenger, for: editing this manuscript, improving upon my writing skills, and working extra long hours to help me meet a deadline for publication.

Thank you, Barry Young and Sterling Thompson for: generous sharing of information and resources to speed up this publication.

Thank you to all the people whose stories I share with the reader, including Ken, Barb, Cia, Mom and Dad, and Paul.

Thank you to all the clients and seminar participants over the last ten years who have asked when I was going to write a book and reach beyond the limited arena of physical therapy. Here it is!

7 Keys To Changing Any Attitude Or Circumstance In Your Life

by Linda McNeil

I know change! You bet I do. And I know LOTS of other people who know change whose lives are miracles, too! How impossible it feels at times. How painful change can be. But how exciting!

I bet you know a little something about change yourself or you wouldn't have picked up this book! Either you want to change some aspect of your life, or you have to. You know that some part of your life isn't working, either personal or professional. You have begun to suspect that change is up to you—not the rest of the world, your boss, your spouse, your kids. So, you want to know how! What do you have to do?

What is my life experience that might convince you there are some ideas here that WORK? Well 17 years ago I weighed 200 pounds and my blood pressure was 220/120. (I now weigh 131 pounds and my blood pressure is 104/60. Sometimes it's almost too low!) I was told I would never be off blood pressure medication. I have been—since 1980.

I had more than a slight drinking and prescription-drug problem. In fact, I am an 11+ years recovered alcoholic. Suffice it to say, I nearly lost a business and I did lose a marriage to my addictions. I even went to jail for a DUI and I greatly hurt most of the people in my life. I certainly hurt myself.

In the midst of all this, I had a seemingly successful physical therapy practice, although at one point (1982) I went to an attorney to ask about the possibility of filing bankruptcy. You know what he said? "Put away your plastic and stop spending money you don't have!"

At another time I was in counseling with a wonderful man named Steve. I will never forget what he told me: "To change a habit, you must stop doing two things and start doing one." He asked me how I went from the edge of bankruptcy to selling my physical therapy practice (which I started with $1100 insurance money from an automobile accident) to selling the practice to a public, national corporation after my business had reached yearly revenues of $1,200,000. I stopped spending on credit, stopped being married to someone who spent like I did, and started taking responsibility for my fiscal future! Thank you, Steve. You were important in my life changes.

Do I have it made now? Do I have all of life's answers? Absolutely not! I seem to project that image, to people I work with in sobriety and to people who hear me present at seminars, courses, and training sessions. But I am still learning. I know that at some level we keep growing—mentally, emotionally, spiritually. We are always seeking. The journey is the fun.

The decision to write this book—to move toward becoming a much more widely-known speaker, to build a speaking and writing empire—is one of the most difficult decisions I have made since the incredibly difficult one I made to sell my physical therapy practice. I find I am as much afraid of success (again?!) as of failure. I value my privacy very much, having been single for 15 years. I find that even when I do a seminar and people are all excited and want more, I sort of pull back, go to my hotel room and assume an attitude of "I have given a few tools that work for me. Now it is your job to pick them up and try them out for yourself!" That attitude may have to change.

Do I have the energy and physical strength to give more? One thing is perfectly clear to me: I am on the planet to share talents granted to me by no merit of my own. I am here to serve. So, it is my fervent hope that you will find something in this book to inspire *you* to change just one or two important areas in your life! Or, maybe you are seeking to deal better with imposed change. The Seven Keys will help you either way.

I am privileged to know people who got sober in prison. Many recovering people I know got so far down that they tried suicide as "the ultimate out." I did. I tried suicide three times. If I hadn't been married to my second spouse and he didn't know me better then I knew myself, I wouldn't be here to tell you about it.

People often share with me their desire to change certain patterns of behavior they see in themselves and their relationships. They ask "<u>How</u> do I change?" The following principles and **changes** acronym will help you make positive and constructive changes in your personal and professional life.

7 Keys To Changing Any Attitude Or Circumstance In Your Life

CHOOSE DIFFERENTLY!

This is: "I don't want to continue fat...unhappy...angry...violent...drunk...being always tardy...in hatred...perfectionist... This is uncomfortable and I want to move." This decision also involves admitting and acknowledging at some level: "I chose this." Accepting choice is very hard.

HURT ENOUGH TO WANT TO CHANGE!

Addicts and former fat people call this "hitting bottom." It applies to all areas where change is needed. It might be thoughts or attempts at suicide, threats of loss of job, family, or anything else you value.

ASK FOR HELP and ACCEPT RESPONSIBILITY FOR YOUR CHOICES!

I personally have never known anyone to triumph over either small or large changes without being humbled enough to ask for help, then to accept responsibility for doing all it takes to create a new result. Our culture does not support attitudes of responsibility.

NEVER QUIT!

Negative thoughts and beliefs are such a part of our culture that you must "keep on keeping on" and surround yourself with people and ideas that are positive and inspiring. Faith and trust in your chosen path are also part of not quitting. Many changes are lifestyle changes.

GRAB ONTO THE NEW, LET GO THE OLD!

For change to be real and lasting, you must make a decision, a commitment to let go your old way of thinking, doing, being, living. You can't hold the old and the new at the same time. You must let go of the old for space to exist for the new. Letting go is harder than grabbing on.

EMBRACE A NEW WAY!

Find JOY in it to persist! It is just like starting an exercise or aerobic program: Find an exercise you truly enjoy to do it enthusiastically for longer than two weeks! You must find something that is fun for you in the long haul.

STOP PLAYING VICTIM!

No one did this to you--despite how much you want to believe your parents or the past or whatever did it to you. Even if you truly were victimized, *today is today* and you must decide to leave the past in the past. How? Apply these 7 Keys. Then:

*Serve others. Surround yourself with positive,
Supportive people who Share your dream!*

There is one thing you always choose....your attitude!

There is one thing you always can change...your attitude!

THE NATURE OF CHANGE

A common reaction to change is *fear!* We seldom give much thought to change until our pain is great, change just comes or we feel change is being forced upon us by no apparent choice of our own. Let us consider what we truly know about change:

Change is inevitable. Until we are buried in the cold hard ground, change will continue. Something in our lives will always be changing—body, mind, spirit, soul, society, the earth, the weather, technology, et al.

Some people have a harder time adapting to change than others. When I do team building with client companies and their employees, I frequently utilize a powerful personality profile called the DiSC^{tm} from the Carlson Learning Company in Minneapolis, Minnesota. This profile reveals the individuals' strengths, weaknesses, and tendencies under stress or when dealing with change. The profile helps clients and their employees see that change is okay and that each person adapts to change in his or her own way and time. Following are the four types of personalities:

- **Dominant** personalities crave and need change, like life blood. They don't always consider all the ramifications of change; therefore their course is frequently not well thought out and, therefore, does not bring the best results.

- **Inducers/Influencers** also love change. They need it and thrive upon it, but they are a lot more people-oriented than task-oriented. Their approach is more team-driven, along the lines of "come on, Team, WE can do it."

6

- **Steadiers** are not particularly fond of change. They need a lot of time and information ahead of time to process how change will affect them and their jobs. They accept change if they have time, information, and can see reason(s) to change.

- **Conscientious** personalities like change the least of all four styles. They have a serious need to do details and their jobs perfectly. Change greatly threatens their status quo. They need to have things "right." They need a lot of guidance and detailed information about why and how in order to make transition. It is helpful if they are involved in the decision-making process.

Even for people who crave and say they love change, change is stressful after a certain point. If you self-administer one of the many stress indices available, you will see high points given for losses and even for changes that most people consider positive, such as marriage and moving; there is still stress associated with loss of the old way.

Most of us did not learn much about the mechanics of "change" at home or in school, so we are pretty uncomfortable with change and don't necessarily know how to change positively and creatively.

FEAR is a typical initial reaction to the idea of change, whether imposed by or from an outside source, or whether you are deciding to change yourself for one reason or another. WHY DO WE FEAR? We fear the unknown. I believe that if we took all our troubles and piled them in front of us, then went wandering around the planet looking to take over someone else's preferably smaller pile, we eventually would come back to our own pile of troubles because we already know how to do them! We are familiar with our own problems and life issues. The unfamiliar is more scary and uncomfortable than what we already know.

Most of us spend most of our lives waiting for someone else to change so *we* will be happier, more free, richer, or whatever. We truly would prefer that the rest of the world change *first!*

We cannot change anyone else. You may think you can, but you can't. In my seminar "**Management by 100% Responsibility**," I ask participants if they have ever been able to change another human being. Once in a while I get a young newlywed or other relationship neophyte who truly believes s/he has changed the new partner. Another person only changes when s/he CHOOSES to change—ideas, behaviors, whatever—to his or her *own benefit, and when and how s/he decides to internalize it for self. We cannot change anyone but ourselves.*

We can, indeed, make it worthwhile for another person to change—when we are willing to change ourselves at the same time. It works like this: If you want the other person to be on time, you MODEL that behavior by being on time yourself. You explain why it is important to you to be on time and to have the other person be on time. You request that he or she also value being on time and consider doing so. Chances are pretty good the other person will decide to try that change. But you cannot *make* the person do it.

To me, being on time for an appointment demonstrates respect for the other person. His or her time is as important as mine is to me. It is a matter of honesty, integrity, and intention.

I had a friend whose time was always so much more important than mine (and I charge well for mine!). She was constantly 30 to 45 minutes late, or more—even for lunch. My value system doesn't tolerate that. She chose not to change. She could have started earlier; returned that last phone call later; respected my time. I ended the relationship.

Parents often think they can change their children. They attempt to do so. They can make it worthwhile for a child to modify a behavior. However, if the child's change is not an internal and personal choice, the child will only *perform* the behavior when the parent is watching and enforcing same. The new behavior will last only when the internal motivation is strong and positive enough. The child initiates and persists in a new behavior *out of personal motivation and need.*

We admire people who truly change their lives and keep them changed! We love stories about "winners" who turn their lives around, do something seemingly impossible or heroic—such as overcome an addiction, recover from cancer, triumph in spite of very difficult circumstances.

Truly effective and long-lasting change never comes from outside of self. CHANGE IS AN INSIDE JOB. Someone else may make it worthwhile by saying: "Change or lose your job...Change or I will leave the marriage...Etc." But true change is internal and is *an individual choice.*

The one thing you can always *choose* is your ATTITUDE.
The one thing you can always *change* is your ATTITUDE!

Now let us examine the hows and whys of change. The following seven chapters will help you. If you feel the need to alter or make something different in your life—a circumstance, belief, attitude, situation, etc.—My best to you. I do not have all the answers. I don't even understand all the questions. However, I have had much experience with *CHOICES and CHANGES and this has empowered me! May you also be empowered!*

9

KEY # 1:   CHOOSE DIFFERENTLY

For Key #1—choosing differently—to begin to work for you, you first must deal with the issue of *choice*. When I was fat, there were many mornings I got up and decided "This is the day! I don't want to be size 22 any longer. I hate myself this way."

I have been on more types of diets than I can remember! I even tried that awful liquid protein diet that killed people in the 1970's by making their hearts go electrically haywire! At the time, I didn't realize that I chose to be fat. It wasn't a conscious or knowing choice.

What is the magical turning point? When do you arrive at the day when you really mean you are ready for change—THIS IS TRULY THE BOTTOM OF THE BARREL? *Webster's Dictionary* defines change as "shift, movement, transformation, transition, alter, make different." When does our transition truly begin?

If you are being abused, hopefully you arrive at a realization like this: "I am out of excuses for leaving...for believing if I act differently s/he will react differently. I deserve better." You choose to do whatever it will take to obtain a different result, a better result. You decide.

If you are angry and negative and want to be more positive and peaceful, one day you say, "I am not happy. This is not a good way to spend the short days of my life. This *IS* my life and I don't want to live it like this any more!" You then are choosing a different way.

If you have been blaming your family, the past, the government, the boss, the kids, the weather, whatever, for all your misery and problems, one day you look around and see someone who is happy and taking charge of the results in his or her life. BINGO! You get it. That's it. Time to move on. Time to let go. Time to forgive. You are choosing a different way.

ONLY you know when you have had enough of your problem. Hence only you can decide to choose a different way. CHOICE is hard. Too bad that it is first, because it might lose a lot of people. Oh well, you gotta want to change BAD! So, get it out of the way. Make choices early in the change process! It works like this:

Webster's Dictionary says **choose** is: "opt for, select, decide, pick, take one thing in preference to another." **Choice** is: "opportunity of choosing, selection." Abraham Lincoln said, "most people are about as happy as they make up their minds to be." I say my life is easy for me when everything is working: my professional life is productive, the marriage is satisfying and solid, the finances are doing well, the investments are earning a fine return. I say, "Yes, I made these choices. I am proud of them. I accept the credit. I'd like a raise, pat on the back, my own private office. Yes, I did that! I will happily take the credit for my choices. I made great choices!"

However, when the marriage falls apart, I am being abused, I am sick, miserable, broke, addicted, in jail, my first reaction is: "It's *not MY fault!!!* It's yours, his, hers, mom's, dad's, the IRS, the ex-wife, the past, the future, the boss, God, Satan, the government, the kids ... ad infinituum!"

It is just human nature to blame others. Most specifically, in this litigious culture of 1997, basically we have all been taught that nothing is our fault. Or, in some families, maybe we were taught that *everything* is our fault, in which case we probably still were not taught the difference among *fault* (error, defect,

11

delinquency); *blame* (condemnation, culpability); and/or *responsibility* (reliability, accountability).

Choose does not necessarily mean **wish** or **want.** IT JUST MEANS *CHOOSE.* Sometimes I make choices that I do not absolutely know if I choose this I will automatically get a given, known, or specific result. Choosing doesn't mean knowing.

For instance, if I choose to smoke, it definitely is a choice. No one else is making me smoke. I decide to buy the cigarettes, then I smoke them. I probably do that because I am cool, I think smoking is cool, I want to fit in and I am infallible, meaning ageless, and I believe that I will be the one never to get lung cancer or emphysema or chronic obstructive pulmonary disease. Victim? Accident? Bad luck? No. Choice. A casually made choice, without any results in mind except the rewards of the moment. So, I choose to smoke, not necessarily wishing, wanting, or knowing whether it will cause cancer.

Where is the choice in divorce if you want to keep your marriage and your partner wants to end it? Obviously, your first choice was to get married. Even if there was a factor like pregnancy, you still had other choices, options, alternatives. With any other personal relationship, there are always choices, options, possibilities, alternatives. The problem is most of us have been taught one way to think, to do, to view what is "right." Therefore, we don't recognize all of our choices.

*Did you know that **right** isn't an absolute concept? **Right** is merely what I say that you agree with. Somebody else hears me and it is **wrong** to them, based on their set of life experiences, learned values, and beliefs.*

Possibly you were brought up in a church that taught you their way absolutely is the only "right" way. Your church and my church may have used the same Book but concluded something totally different from its contents; that is, "*Our* way is the only "right" way! You don't do things this way, you will go to hell, be punished, or burn, or whatever." Can we all be absolutely "right"—using the same book?

Let's get back to the marriage that is falling apart. The initial choice (conscious or unconscious) was to get married or not to get married. Then there was a series of choices (conscious or unconscious): stay married or not, be happy or unhappy; be faithful or unfaithful (we don't just happen into affairs), go to counselling or not, go to church or not, have children or not, etc. One of the frightening things in our society is that we seem to think these things just sort of *happen TO* us. It is *NOT* that way.

Now let's talk about some of the really tough issues. Do we *choose* abuse or disease? Or are we victims of a sick society, a sick world, a sick family? Does terminal illness just happen to us, or is it the fault of our parents, our genetics? Remember, choosing does not necessarily mean wishing or wanting, it just means choosing.

Sometimes we do not know what our choices are until we get clear on the concept that we have choices. Other times we choose unknowingly. It is important to leave out blame, shame and guilt.

Does the child with leukemia choose the disease? How can a child choose abuse? Well, there are people that you and I know who believe in truly 100% responsibility; they believe in the concept of reincarnation and, therefore, believe that they even choose their parents (for a lesson to be learned in this lifetime). I haven't arrived at that understanding, but I try to keep my mind open. I do know there are times when it seems disease just "happens" by no act of our own. When I get really honest, I can see some of the choices that may have contributed to the underlying or even active *causes thereof*. They may have been

13

knowing or unknowing choices, consciously or unconsciously made.

Even if true victimization does exist and the world truly is a terrible place, or God is a vengeful God or the Devil plays dirty tricks on us... or whatever is or might be your belief system, even if we cannot get to an analytical understanding of causes and choices, we are left with the choices that make up our lives *after the horrible happening or victimization.*

If you were sexually or physically abused, at what point are you willing to CHOOSE YOUR REACTION DIFFERENTLY and stop allowing victimization to continue affecting and determining your happiness or unhappiness today?

If you are dealing with a terminal disease, what might have been or what might be the choices facing you today? Say you chose to smoke; or to travel to unknown parts of the world and eat possibly contaminated or polluted food or water; or you unknowingly put yourself at risk for a particular cancer. I AM NOT SAYING you got up one day, decided your life was a bit boring and said, "I think I will choose cancer." I am saying you might have chosen certain high-risk behaviors that put you in a position to <u>not do all it takes to protect yourself against cancer</u>.

You may not agree or even understand all I've said about choice (unless you have been exposed to this thinking in the past). My intention here is to upset your usual way of seeing the world! I invite you out of your "brain-box" and want to inspire you to open your mind to see things in perhaps a different way!

If you have a terminal disease and can't see that you made any choices to cause it, *all that matters now is the series of choices you are currently making to deal with this reality NOW.* I am *not* saying that if you have an advanced case of cancer, you can just decide to not have it. In a most real sense, that would be

14

dangerous denial. However, there are people who believe that the mind is so powerful as to be able to heal anything, with the help of a Higher Power.

101 CHOICES WE ALL MAKE

1. Who we are
2. Who we love
3. Who we become
4. Who we help
5. Who we hang out with
6. Who we work with
7. Who we play with
8. Who we work for
9. Who we travel with
10. Who we support
11. Who we listen to
12. Who we share ourselves with
13. Who we marry
14. Who we don't marry
15. Who we have as friends
16. What we do with our lives
17. What career(s) we choose
18. What job(s) we take
19. What we are
20. What we love
21. What we love to do
22. What we think
23. What we spend our time on
24. What we believe in
25. What our lives look like
26. What we relate to
27. What we put in our minds
28. What we read
29. What we watch on television
30. What we listen to
31. What we feel
32. What we participate in
33. What we contribute to

34. When we grow up
35. When we leave the past behind
36. When we marry
37. When we work
38. When we play
39. When we love
40. When we hate
41. When we are happy
42. When we are unhappy
43. When we participate in life
44. When we don't participate in life
45. When we *do* anything
46. When we think good thoughts
47. When we think bad thoughts
48. Where we live
49. Where we don't live
50. Where we play
51. Where we work
52. Where we travel
53. Where we don't travel
54. Where we do anything
55. Why we love
56. Why we hate
57. Why we do or choose any of the above
58. Why we think the thoughts we think
59. Why we work
60. Why we play
61. How we work
62. How we play
63. How we make love
64. How we love
65. How we express ourselves
66. How we grow spiritually
67. How we *don't* grow spiritually
68. How we think
69. How we dress
70. How we drive
71. How we look
72. How we do sports
73. How we participate in life

74. How we *don't* participate in life
75. How we do friendship
76. How we share
77. How we *don't* share
78. How happy we are
79. How unhappy we are
80. How friendly we are
81. How courteous we are
82. How angry we are
83. How peaceful we are
84. How much we share
85. How much we make
86. How much we travel
87. How much we love
88. How much we contribute
89. How much we work
90. How much we play
91. How much we know
92. How much we *don't* know
93. How much we care
94. How much we live
95. How much we die
96. How much we want
97. How much we are grateful for
98. How much we are willing to do
99. How much we are willing to give
100. How much we believe in something
101. How much of a difference we make in our lifetime.

"You don't get to choose how you're going to die or when. You can only decide how you're going to live."
Joan Baez

KEY # 2: HURT ENOUGH TO WANT TO CHANGE

There all types of pain—physical, mental, spiritual, social. Let's surmise that your life is comprised of work, home, family life, play, spiritual, and whatever else. If any part of your life is miserable or painful enough, at some point you come to recognize the pain as something you are not willing to live with anymore. Then you begin to choose differently.

When I drank, I would get up in the morning and decide not to drink, or only have one at lunch, or two or four at "twofers-time." I was a terrible liar. I never did what I said. Once I started, I couldn't stop or control the amount I drank. My behavior was crazy. I hurt myself and others. I went to jail. Yet, the outside world saw a "successful" woman, owner of a small business, with all the "trappings."

Here is my personal "hitting-bottom" story: It was January, 1980. I got on the scales, and tipped it at 200 pounds. I am five feet four. That means I was wearing size 22. I WAS FAT! My brother was getting married and I had a very hard time finding a petite, fat dress for the wedding. I still carry a picture of me sitting at the wedding. I did not look very happy.

My then husband and I lived in a big, four-bedroom house on a hill. We had a large yard, waterfalls, and lovely pools. The house was furnished well. From the outside, it looked as though we had the perfect life. We had snowmobiles, motorcycles, and numerous expensive toys. I drove a jazzy little Datsun 280ZX.

I tried suicide three times. I hated myself. My business was struggling (it got worse later!); I had 35 employees whose children I worried about feeding. My marriage was just a

18

marriage—not necessarily happy, not necessarily unhappy. My husband did just about anything to keep me and the lifestyle going. We spent a LOT of money—eating out at night, drinking, playing, generally living the "high" life and impressing others. We had no savings and no investments. We spent it all!

When I got on the scales, and saw **200 pounds**, I looked in the mirror and actually saw my red eyes, broken blood vessels on my cheeks, the horrible gray color of my skin—the color of pewter! I said to myself "What the hell is wrong with you? You have everything. I hate you! I hate my body. I hate myself. I am miserable." I couldn't seem to die, and I couldn't seem to live. I needed help.

My sister-in-law was in town and my husband and I were meeting her for lunch. I sat down and said "I think I'm an alcoholic. I need help." My husband nearly fell off his chair. (As though he didn't know!) My sister-in-law said, "That's the best news I've heard in a long time. I hope you know your family loves you very much and will stand by you no matter what." God, what a miracle! And they did, to the best of their ability and understanding of what we all came to know as the disease of alcoholism.

I went to the doctor (I used to go to the doctor a LOT, and to the hospital at least yearly, whether I needed it or not). The nurse said, "What is it THIS time, Lin?" The doctor said, "That's great, we will help you. Let's get you admitted as soon as possible." Thus began one of the most amazing and challenging journeys of my life. I would not trade it for all the gold on the planet, because I have witnessed miracle after miracle. Mine is one of the small ones!

I only know that for me I reached enough pain. My clothes didn't fit. The three suicide attempts didn't work. The lonely space in my head was expanding. The hole in my soul was so big there wasn't enough of anything to fill it. I suspected that I had "hit bottom" and **I hurt enough to *WANT* to change.**

Hitting bottom can apply to anything—mental or emotional state of mind, physical condition, spiritual condition, drinking, drugging, abuse, et al. Others might think they are being helpful when they try to get you to deal with an obvious problem, but until the pain is great enough, you do not recognize the "bottom." This also applies to "small" issues.

With addictions, it is said that sometimes the bottom rises up to meet you. This means that some people lose everything—family, home, job(s), self-respect, money, stability, stuff, perhaps go to prison or an insane asylum—before they "hit bottom." No one else can determine how low "bottom" is before it gets our attention. We can even go as far as death.

Some people *choose* to get off the sinking elevator before it reaches the absolute bottom. The pain might be enough when something relatively minor happens. Perhaps the boss says something, or the spouse relates an embarrassing incident, or a blackout gets the person in trouble or just scares him or her. Or the person may see the bottom coming when the doctor says, "Quit smoking, quit drinking, lose weight or you're going to die." *ONLY THE PERSON WITH THE PAIN KNOWS WHEN HE OR SHE HAS HIT BOTTOM!*

A 40-something male friend of mine was having some physical problems and went to a doctor. The diagnosis was diabetes. He had been drinking heavily, was overweight, and was having other difficulties. I asked my friend how he was able to simply make a decision then DO IT. (I really wanted to know was if he was at bottom.) He said that when the doctor told him his diabetes could be treated with daily medication, change of diet, weight loss and exercise, it became instantly clear to him that if he wanted to stay alive, he must comply. His most meaningful motivator was the need to watch his kids grow up and to be part of their lives. Amazingly, he stopped drinking, lost weight, began playing golf and working out on a regular basis. Today, he looks and feels entirely different.

That tells me he had not yet crossed the invisible line from casual or social drinking to the disease of alcoholism. Many alcoholics, when told by their doctors that they absolutely cannot take another drink **or they will die,** simply still cannot stop drinking. They have not yet reached a sufficiently painful "bottom." Certainly in some instances, the doctor telling an alcoholic "STOP OR DIE" may be their hitting bottom. The point is: *NO ONE ELSE CAN KNOW WHEN YOU HAVE HAD ENOUGH PAIN. Only you can choose to change and end the pain.*

If "hurt enough to want to change" does not make sense to you yet, you have not reached the limit of your pain—and you may not be ready to change.

However, if you understand "hurt enough" and you are in enough pain that you really WANT to change, you are well on your way! You have a serious *need   or   desire* to change. How can you know for sure that you are ready? Go back to your old behavior; if the pain returns in sufficient force, it is not going to disappear on its own! *You* must help it!

A woman friend of mine decided to lose weight, for real. I had watched her doing what I did over and over: go on a diet, exercise, lose weight, gain it back; Go on a diet, exercise, lose weight, gain it back. I asked her what made her finally decide to go to Weight Watchers and lose 35 pounds. She said she "hit bottom" one day when she bent over to tie her shoe laces and could hardly reach them. Her emotional pain was strong enough that the magic happened. "THIS IS IT!" she declared. Since Weight Watchers, she has kept off most of the weight; she is now a competitive bicycle rider. I admire her very much. She rides for charities and she maintains a highly successful career as a stock broker. She is my broker, in fact, for which I am quite fortunate and grateful!

The 7 Keys in this book will also work for less drastic and obvious choices to change. Not all changes need be as dramatic as that of addicts--*because not everyone has to hurt that bad!* The point is that if people in dire straits can do amazing about-faces, you certainly can use these keys to change habits like perfectionism, being late, constant criticism, anger, being judgmental, feeling disgusted or unhappy.

If there is a behavior pattern in your relationships which you have tried to change and you know it costs you friendships, you may experience sufficient discomfort to get serious about *wanting* to change. Many people have a serious desire to be involved in a romantic relationship. They will get into one and are madly in love for several months while everything is perfect, dreamy, and idealistic. Then they start seeing all kinds of things wrong with the other not-so-perfect person. They begin criticizing. The other person, who began as lovely and nurturing now is like a totally different person!

What happened? How can you change such a problem? How can you change resistance to a truly intimate and whole relationship? Beginning to change the pattern is being willing to launch the next "key." You ask for help and accept responsibility for your choices!

Others can stop you temporarily,
only you can do it permanently.
Dr. Robert Anthony

22

CHANGE YOUR THINKING—

CHANGE YOUR LIFE!

KEY #3: ASK FOR HELP AND ACCEPT RESPONSIBILITY FOR YOUR CHOICES

No matter what you want to change in your life—something that has cost you, caused some difficulty or pain, someone has been there before you! Someone has written a book. Or there is a self-help group. Or your neighbor knows someone who has been just about where you are. Or you might want to seek the help of a professional counselor. There is already a vast body of knowledge to help you positively change!

One of the hardest parts of changing yourself or something about your life, is the feeling that no one else has had exactly your same circumstances...past history...problem. This belief alienates you from the help you want and can find. You find yourself terribly alone deep in your heart. *Asking for help is absolutely essential to begin the mechanics of change.*

1) Asking for help is humbling. That's a good starting place to build a healthy self-esteem.

2) Asking for help creates a connection to others who have been down your path before you. Relatedness is necessary for mutual support and information-sharing. You literally *learn* what to do.

3) Asking for help opens your eyes and ears.

4) Asking for help begins with opening your heart and mind.

If weight loss is your goal, here is what to do: First, you admit to your innermost self that you are fat...that you indeed need help. That is humbling. That is a beginning. Next, you go to a support group, such as Weight Watchers. (They have a great reputation for helping thousands of people turn their lives around.) On arrival, you look around and see many people of all sizes, shapes and places of progress in their weight loss. Some are at the beginning--just like you! Many are much fatter! Some don't even look like they belong there. (they are the ones returning to check in, to remember what they were and to what they will return if they don't remain vigilant!).

The other fat members rush to share their stories with you. They have learned that *they* make more progress by sharing their experiences, strength, and hope. That is why you're there! By listening, you learn what to do, how long it takes to change your habits, what it will feel like when you actually see the new thin, *real* you emerge!

I can answer that one fairly accurately. When I lost my first 40 pounds in 1980, I was in the San Diego area, on the "island" of Coronado. I was running one day and some guy whistled at me! I was so shocked I nearly ran right into a car! Shortly after, I was sitting in a Jacuzzi at the apartment complex where I was staying for the summer. A gorgeous young guy from the Navy started flirting outrageously with me. I remember going back to the apartment, thinking "These guys are really sick. What is wrong with them?" Then I looked in the mirror and was struck by what I saw. I looked great! WOW! I'd not been seeing what the rest of the world was seeing. I'd been seeing fat!

ASKING FOR HELP IS NECESSARY AND ESSENTIAL!

The truth is that it probably doesn't especially matter WHO you ask for help! You can ask:

- God, or whatever you believe is a Power
  higher than you
- Your best friend
- Your teacher
- Your family, spouse, kids
- A counselor
- A minister or spiritual guide
- A group (self-help or otherwise)
- Even an enemy.

So, do it. Ask for help. Go to the library. Go to a minister, counselor, psychiatrist, doctor, friend, support group, organization, your lover, mother, father, spouse.

Most of us don't know how to ask for help. We have the idea we shouldn't have to ask, that either others will see our pain or problems and offer to help... or offer a solution... or rescue us... or whatever it is you were brought up to believe. OR we believe *we* are supposed to have all the answers, know how to handle everything. OR we just are not willing to appear unknowing or vulnerable. That is one of my favorites. I am a small woman who succeeded fairly well in the world of "men in business." Not true, but that's how I saw it. So, if I admitted that I didn't know something—or that I needed help—or didn't know where to get answers or what to do next—someone might take advantage of me, hurt me, get to me!

One of my big lessons about asking for help came in early 1996. I had been hiking a lot. My knee began to hurt seriously when I came down a steep trail. I finally decided to go to a doctor and ended up with a well-known orthopedist. He was "95% sure" that I needed an arthroscopy due to a problem with a meniscus, very likely from horseback riding, falls, and a history of tumbling team falls, in high school. This simple procedure should be able to correct the problem and I could get on with hiking and all the rest.

Talk about interesting choices. I previously had chosen a cheap insurance when my COBRA ran out and I no longer had corporate coverage. I ended up in a mobile, day-surgery setting; they had no laser, which, as it turned out, could have helped greatly. Instead of a repairable meniscus problem, the doctor found severe arthritis. Without a laser to scrape and cause enough "damage" to create some bleeding and tissue damage so that new, healthier tissue would form, basically nothing could be done.

I had been meeting a group of mutually-supportive women on Wednesday nights. Before the surgery I told them what was happening. I was very upset when no one called to check on me and ask how I was doing. The next week, when my friend, Mo, called to see if I was attending the group, I said "No." I was pretty disgusted that no one cared enough to call. I will not soon forget Mo's reply: "Gee, Lin, let's think about that. What you did was show up smiling, as usual, acting as though everything was handled and under control. You seemed absolutely OK with it all." I said, "Everything is NOT all right. I needed your support! How am I supposed to get it?!" My loving friend said "Perhaps you could ask for support when you need it!" Perhaps.

Now comes the hard part: accepting responsibility for our choices. In recovery from addictions, there is an interesting phenomenon. Many addicts and alcoholics come from very religious backgrounds and attempt to address their alcoholism, addictions, and issues by returning to the church or religion of their childhood. Then they can't figure out why—if God or a Higher Power is required for recovery—the church didn't work? In my opinion and by my long-term observation, as wonderful as the grace of God is, unless and until recovering persons take

responsibility for the messes they have made of their lives, jobs, marriages, finances, health, past and present, all the grace in the universe will not solve their problems nor move them into recovery.

So—if you accept that no matter what it is that you want to change, you did something to cause it by putting yourself in that position—knowingly or unknowingly, consciously or unconsciously—and you realize that you must do all it takes to create a different result, then you are accepting personal responsibility for your life and choices. HOW DO YOU FOLLOW-THROUGH? Accepting responsibility means doing *ALL* it takes to create a different result.

When I weighed 200 pounds and wanted to lose 70, I wanted to just *think* differently or *pray* myself thin. You know what? No matter how much I prayed, God never did come down and push me away from the table or run me around the block or lift the weights for me! I could not *just* diet ... or *just* pray ... *just* exercise ... or just *think* differently ... or *do* differently for a short period of time. That's why Richard Simmons calls it a "live-it," not a diet. A life change means doing ALL it takes for as long as it takes to create a different result. Most cases of desired change means for the rest of our lives!

I was privileged to participate with my dear mother in her recovery from cancer. There was a point in her disease when she made a conscious decision to do all it would take to recover. She would not give up. When looking out over the canyon in the backyard, near the beautiful San Isabel National Forest in southern Colorado, she decided that she had the love of her family and a life worth living and she was not about to give up until she was ready. She decided then to do all it would take for the best possibility of recovery.

28

That meant having surgery to remove the diseased part of her body, then a radiation implant, which has had difficult side effects such as stomach and intestinal problems. Her recovery to normalcy has been long and slow. She is constantly vigilant and takes the best care of herself she can. She has had to adopt new behaviors. I asked her to try something else new to her—mental imaging, to mentally visualize the "good" white cells gobbling up the "bad" cancer cells. Many fervent prayers were said on her behalf, also. And the miracle happened.

Was, is it all worth it? Yes. At the times when she suffers the side effects of the radiation, I know she wonders whether it is worth it. However, being the person she is, I don't believe she would have done differently.

My Mom recently brought her 93-year-old mother into her own 52-year-old marriage, to live with them. My parents added a room to their home to accommodate Grandma during her last years. My Mom is finding strength she—and we—didn't know she had. She continues to accept responsibility for her own recovery and ongoing health.

My father has had his recovery issues as well. He was seriously burned when he was to go jeeping with Mom and friends. The jeep wouldn't start. Mom cranked the starter while Dad threw gasoline on the carburetor. The gasoline exploded, and Dad tossed the can into the air. Gasoline came down all over him, burning 20-25% of his upper body with second and third degree burns. He was wearing a polyester jumpsuit which melted to him. He rolled on the ground to put out the fire. Most definitely, my Dad did not knowingly cause this accident. No one else did it to him, either. Blame is not the issue. The accident seems to have been the result of unconscious actions or choices without proper caution and forethought to possible consequences.

Dad made great choices with the event of the accident. He rolled on the ground; went to the hospital; took the medicine, the physical therapy, and whirlpools; and got the skin grafts. Going to visit my Dad and seeing him in terrible pain is an experience I never want again. Burns are horrible! I will never forget the smell of his burned flesh. My Mom will never forget the sight of him on fire.

My Dad certainly had to ask for help and accept responsibility for his actions. Today he is a very active 75-year-old! He still tills his gardens, wrestles calves, and throws hay bales.

Asking for help and accepting responsibility for my own choices was pivotal and crucial. When I was early in alcohol recovery and still working in my physical therapy practice, I discovered that I had been embezzled and was in financial trouble. Talk about more interesting choices! I had not been reading my own financial statements regularly; I was not even signing the corporate checks or paychecks myself. The only time I had information about the corporation's financial status was when my bookkeeper/accountant prepared a financial statement for me to take to the bank to sign personally for a loan.

I was dealing with some pretty sizable reimbursement problems, both in the rehab agency and the home health agency. I had a second lien on my home and didn't know where to turn. An attorney I met said, "Bankruptcy is not the answer to your problems. Here is the reality: You will not be keeping that nice diamond on your finger. You will not be driving that lovely sports car. You will not be living in that nice house on the hill. My advice is: Stop spending like there is no tomorrow. Go home and tear up your credit cards. Start saving. Live differently and take responsibility for your finances." Good advice. Thank you, John. I took his advice.

My husband was an over-spender, too. That also came to an end. We were both used to large salaries and huge benefits. We had no savings and had barely started an IRA for retirement. We were used to spending it ALL.

Another significant consultant also helped me turn my finances around. The CPA asked me, "How do you spend all you make?" I didn't even understand the question! "What do you mean?" I asked. "We buy toys, cars, houses, eat out a lot, travel a lot, play a lot." I don't understand what happened in my brain. I know my parents were savers, so I must have grown up around that kind of thinking. I know they were appalled by the way my husband and I blew all our money!

I stopped doing two things: over-spending and spending money I didn't have. I stopped being married to a man who did the same. I began taking responsibility for my own financial future. I began investing in my own retirement, even when I thought I couldn't afford it.

The CPA had a huge impact on my life. Dave taught me to read the Wall Street Journal. He taught me to protect the business from embezzlement. He led me into knowing that having money is not evil. He walked me through deal-making and selling my business. Thank you, Dave.

Where am I now financially? I am in a solid-enough monetary position to work part-time, learn new skills, write a book, and record tapes. Writing a book costs money and I can loan myself the money.

How are you doing? What do you need help with? Better communication with your children, spouse, family? Ending of a relationship? Anger, resentment, fear? Abuse, drugs, alcohol? A business venture, an old job, a new job? Friends, lovers, money? The past, present, future?

For what do you need to accept responsibility? Your marriage? Your money? Your past? *I* don't know the answer. You do. You can do *all* it takes to create a different result. You can create positive change!

Asking for help and taking responsibility are not just a one-time accomplishment. You can't just take responsibility for your marriage... or your anger... or your weight... today (only.) While, it is true that today is the only day you can change, taking responsibility means changing every single day. For good. Forever. That attitude and behavior brings the final successful result.

The good news is: **One day at a time is all you can do and *anybody* can change one habit for one day!** Those single days add up to a *changed habit*. I have heard that to change a habit we only need to change how we do something SEVEN times! Well, I have no empirical or scientific evidence to substantiate that, but if we drive to work a different route seven trips in a row, we are well on our way to creating a new habit of driving to work. Maxwell Maltz says it takes 21 days to establish a new habit.

That is basically how we accept responsibility for our choices. We clean up our pasts after acknowledging that we made choices that put us where we are today. Then we do all we can *one day at a time* to change the results. When we want to reduce our weight, we make a life style change forever—one day at a time. To change being habitually late, we accept the consequences of our past behavior, learn new behaviors, we do *all* it takes to change and live differently every day.

Webster's Dictionary says responsibility is being reliable, trustworthy, stable. Sometimes responsibility is merely the *"ability to respond."*

In Colorado we periodically have major hail storms. I have experienced two such destructive storms in my years as a homeowner. I have had to replace the shake shingles of two homes, re-paint both homes and make other numerous repairs due to the severity of these summer disasters. Perhaps you have had the same experience. If your responsibility is to clean up after a hail storm, even though you'd rather not, if you choose to live in an area where hail storms happen often, responsibility is the ability to respond after a hail storm.

Any system which takes responsibility
away from people, dehumanizes them.
Dr. Robert Anthony

RESPONSIBILITY:

ABILITY TO RESPOND.

POSITIVELY.

KEY #4: NEVER QUIT!

The path of least resistance is giving up. The world and society often don't want us to succeed. We are taught much negativity. We have heard a lot more about what we can't do than what we **_can_** do.

The world's greatest feats have been accomplished by very persistent people as noted in "Chicken Soup for the Soul" by Mark V. Hansen and Jack Canfield:

♦ Babe Ruth, considered by many to be one of the greatest athletes of all time, is famous for setting the home run record. He also struck out 1330 times.
♦ Eighteen publishers turned down Richard Bach's 10,000 word story about a "soaring" seagull, *Jonathan Livingston Seagull*. Macmillan finally published it in 1970. By 1975, it had sold over seven million copies in the U.S. alone.
♦ Henry Ford went broke five times before he finally succeeded.
♦ Winston Churchill failed sixth grade. When he was 62 he became the prime minister of England after a lifetime of defeats. He made his greatest contributions as a "senior citizen."

DON'T QUIT!

KEEP GOING!

I wanted dieting to be a one-time event! It isn't! I have surrendered to the fact that watching my diet and exercising is forever—just as all the other improvements in my life. If I think, "I can **never** drink again... never eat what I want again... never be in love again," I am overwhelmed and incredibly discouraged. The only successful way to do any change is:

- Make a decision.
- Practice, practice, practice.
- Apply all the other things we have discussed above and that come after this.
- Do each new behavior and way of thinking *one day at a time!*

Forever is too long for our minds to grasp. We can handle one day at a time.

To keep going, get rid of your negative thoughts and beliefs. Your family may have taught you to not get your hopes up, so you wouldn't be disappointed—or some such thing. Our culture reinforces the negative and minimizes the positive. IT'S UP TO YOU TO MAXIMIZE THE POSITIVE.

For evidence of that, all you have to do is turn on the news. Some newscasts think that one small piece of *good news* (e.g., five minutes out of two hours) is enough. When I catch myself believing that the world really is destroying itself, I stop listening to the news. If we go to war or the stock market crashes and I go broke, I figure someone will let me know.

Thinking positive is a big part of any changes we wish to make in our lives. Thinking positive must be accompanied by positive ACTION and surrounding ourselves by positive people. The action is imperative. It involves risk and major effort. Then, we must seek out positive people with great striving, focused effort, and clear choice. There *are* more people getting positive! They

35

understand **"Change your thinking, change your life!"** I choose to spend my time with positive thinkers and action types. They understand positive acts and random acts of kindness. They truly produce immense and significant changes on this planet. And you can, too!

To keep going, to inspire you to NEVER QUIT is to surround yourself with inspirational books and movies. Find material that inspires you!

When I need a boost (to get in touch with myself) I go for a hike, preferably in the high country. Hiking up a high mountain trail, where no one but one or two horses and perhaps one other hiker have been all season, puts me in touch with my Authentic Self... lets me know *anything* is possible! *I just have to keep going!!*

Another excellent way to bolster your positive energy is to read great books. I recently read an autobiography about Todd Huston, *More Than Mountains: The Todd Huston Story*. I hope to meet this awesome man some day. He is on my list of 101 goals! At the age of 14, Todd was boating when his legs got caught in the boat propeller. On-going medical problems forced him to choose amputation at the age of 21. It would have been simpler for him—and very acceptable to society—to spend the rest of his life in a wheelchair. Instead, he was obsessed with the desire to overcome mountains, literally and figuratively. He challenged a climbing record held by an able-bodied man. He sought to climb the highest peak in each of the 50 United States (in one hundred days or less!)

He climbed through the pain of a misfit prosthesis, friction irritation, bleeding, and skin problems. His triumph was climbing to the top of Mt. McKinley in Alaska! I have hiked 12 times up to 14,000 feet; easy walk-up Fourteeners. Whenever I feel sorry for myself because at my age *my* little hiking career is probably coming to a close because of severe arthritis in my knees, I think of Todd Huston! He DID IT! I can do it, too! So, I keep hiking!

It helps to surround ourselves with inspiration on every level. As a lover of the outdoors, hiking, and climbing, I recommend the movie, *K-2*, about a 28,000 foot high mountain in the Himalayas. I have probably viewed this movie more than five times. It always thrills, scares, and inspires me!

There is *real power* in knowing that if others can, you can!

A great spiritual principle is *"What I focus on, expands."* If you focus on everything you cannot do, that is all you can see. You just see more and more of what you absolutely cannot do. Self pity sets in.

If you focus on everything you *can* do, THAT is what you see. You then get to live in gratitude and abundance!

You are absolutely where you are supposed to be! You have enough of everything—right now! Tomorrow is a new day. Tomorrow is full of creative solutions—and so are you!

That also applies to the people with whom you surround yourself. I expected my friends and family to say, "What? You can't write a book. Don't be silly." Not one of them, even my CPAs and attorneys, told me I couldn't! Every person said, "Go for it! You can do it!" Wow! I have made good choices in my friends!

> *Whatever you want,*
> *wants you.*
> *Dr. Robert Anthony*

KEY #5: GRAB ON TO THE NEW, LET GO THE OLD

For change to be real and lasting we must make conscious decisions, commitments to let go of old ways of thinking, doing, being, living. Since we cannot hold both the old and the new at the same time, we absolutely must let go of the old in order to create space for new habits, ideas, patterns, and possibilities. Letting go must be completely, without reservation, without doubt.

In the "12-step" community, we often hear, "Anything I finally let go of still has claw marks all over it!" Most of us have a difficult time "letting go." We like our lives familiar and comfortable. We don't want changes we don't understand or know how to do well. When I was in the throes of my alcohol addiction, I didn't want to try anything I was not already good at. I didn't want to be embarrassed. I didn't want to look bad. My sense of humor was stifled! I mean, I was important. I was the Boss. I couldn't laugh at myself.

How I've changed! Today, I don't care who laughs at me. And they do! I am willing to try anything new which excites me, enhances my life, doesn't hurt anyone else and doesn't hurt me. My sense of humor and daring have led me to do some foolhardy things. However, I have learned to let go of the old and grab onto the new. Fun and laughter are a big part of my life today.

Letting go of old ideas, my old way of life, old loves, and my physical therapy practice were very hard releases. I was "married" to my business twice as long as either spouse. The business was my life and my identity. Sometimes I still miss the socialization of the office setting and being needed in the business on a daily basis. The first Christmas without my business it was strange not to be part of deciding what we would do differently than the 16 Christmas celebrations before. Would we be able to pay cash bonuses to employees? Should we do a sleigh ride? Dinner party? Home party? Have gifts? Draw names? I felt totally lost without the big celebration. I had a hard time letting go of the status and connection. I also had a hard time letting go of the income, the steady predictable paycheck. That showed me how much my identity was connected to how much money I made. Even my self-esteem was determined by my paycheck!

Finally I was able to let go of the need to be a boss—the authority and center of my little universe. I moved into a much more solitary situation—a home office. How do you make the decision and transition?

> ⇒ Get clear that letting go is important and indeed necessary.
> ⇒ Ask for help.
> ⇒ Clear mental and emotional space for something new.
> ⇒ Look for something to replace your old way of living, being, doing.

OLD THINGS YOU MIGHT HAVE TO LET GO OF:

♦ Old ideas, such as: "That's just the way it is ... That's the way it has always been ... Because I said so."
♦ Excuses for being the way you are: "That just the way I am! My grandmother was that way ... My father is that way ..."
♦ Old loves. It seems to take at least a year to heal and really let go.
♦ Identity based on expense accounts, position, title.

39

- Job identities. You are more than just a doctor, dentist, secretary, stockbroker, lawyer, business owner, parent, homemaker.
- Identity based on someone else in your life: wife, husband, mother, father.
- Money, things, and their connection to who you are.
- Who everyone else thinks you are or ought to be.
- Past family experiences: for example, you are this way because you were victimized abused, etc.

Al-Anon (a 12 step group for friends and families of alcoholics) tells us that frequently we let go by extending a hand in front of us, palm up with open fingers, stating "I am willing to let go." This reserves an "out" for us. We can close our fingers and take back our old ideas and behaviors whenever we get too uncomfortable.

To let go for good, extend your hand in front of you **palm down,** open your fingers and release downward. Gravity takes over and the ideas, thoughts, and behaviors are gone beyond your ability to take them back. This is "Letting go and Letting God."

No matter what your spiritual belief, to change your personal or business life, it helps to access a Higher Power—whatever that is for you. Frequently there comes a time when you personally have done all you can to improve yourself and your situation and you have to let go again! It is my experience that the grace of God helps in this process. "Be patient," I say to myself—and my friends—"God isn't finished with me yet!"

Selfishness was and still is my very human trait. Personal awareness and growth has taken a lot of effort. It helped me immensely to get busy helping others. During the times of my biggest and most challenging decisions, I often felt sorry for myself. My self-absorption became all consuming. I was all wrapped up in myself.

No one felt sorry for me. And no one would play the pity game with me. To others I appeared to be suddenly wealthy: it is all relative! I had three years of payments and interest coming in, after I sold my business, so I could virtually travel and play. I found that what I focused on, expanded. When I focused on change and loss, I hurt. When I focused on fun and new things, I got to do them.

I did. I learned to scuba dive then took a trip to the Seychelles islands 1000 miles east of Nairobi to learn underwater photography. I fell in love with diving! I swam with an 11-foot gray Whale Shark, learned to night dive, and did my first wreck dive.

My first night dive was a real adventure! On the way to the site a woman shared her first terror-filled night dive story with me. I am sure that didn't help me relax. My dive buddy was also our group leader, my trip roommate, and my photography teacher. She was so confident of my diving skills, that once we entered the dark and disorienting sea, she proceeded to fully engage— taking her own great photos. The problem was that she ignored me—a relative novice. Because of low-back surgery I cannot wear a typical weight belt diving—but have my weights in the pocket of my buoyancy compensator. In my fear and frustration I inadvertently tripped the cord which released the weights, leaving me no ability to stay underwater. After taking a few very nice night photos of anemone "open" and feeding, and numerous wonderfully bright-colored, dark-eyed Squirrel fish, I floated to the surface. There I was out in the middle of the Indian Ocean all by myself in the dark—scared to death! I shouted at the boat operators to help. They shouted back, "What are you doing on the surface?!" I yelled, "I don't know! I don't *want* to be here!" They were not happy with me for losing those weights. Because of the islands' location so far from the mainland, getting sufficient supplies of heavy dive weights is no small feat!

I also experienced my first near-disaster dive in the Seychelles. A divemaster and another newly-certified diver accompanied me through an eight foot diameter tunnel in the granite, on the ocean floor. There was a very strong, difficult serge current that jerks you strongly one direction, stops, then throws you the opposite direction. We caught the serge current, strategically passing through the tunnel into a box-canyon-shaped area. Under the low rocks, sleeping on the ocean floor, was a Nurse shark. I was carrying my camera and got very excited. The divemaster and I were concerned about the new diver and what might be her reaction to a shark. If she panicked, we were in trouble. Although a Nurse shark is virtually harmless, it is still a shark and deserves respect and space. So, we proceeded to take photos, while keeping an eye on the shark *and* the inexperienced diver. It turned out she didn't even realize what we were seeing was a shark! We managed to spook the shark and it swam powerfully in a circle, exiting the box-canyon through the tunnel. My heart was pounding!

I had taken a few good photos and it was time to follow the shark out. I was so thrilled and nervous that I caught the current too high on the way back through the tunnel. The current threw me up against the rock at the top of the tunnel, which caught my air line and held me there. Fortunately, I had on a wet suit (which I seldom wear), and had the presence of mind to duck my head and pull the camera toward my body. That action saved my head and camera from being crushed by the rock. I waited for the current to reverse directions, which allowed me to unhook from the rock and get through the tunnel safely. When I reached the boat, I realized what a close call it was. The divemaster said, "I can't believe you weren't crushed! Look at your tank and wetsuit!" The tank was partially caved-in by crashing against the rock and the wetsuit looked like someone had poured acid on it—small bits had been torn from it. It protected me from serious cuts and scrapes. This was a powerful experience because it assured me that my skills were good and my instincts were perfect for self-preservation. I found this experience very significant in letting go of old ideas and lack of confidence trying new things. I also began to see the importance of becoming willing to "grab onto the new," and the necessity of finding joy doing stimulating, fresh activities. I gained a new awareness that Someone-Up-There was watching over me!

With 22 Americans (12 from Colorado), I went into Kenya on a photography safari in four game parks: Masai Mara Game Reserve (a hot air balloon ride there); Lake Nakuru (hundreds of thousands of brilliantly pink Flamingoes); Buffalo Springs National Reserve; and Samburu Reserve. It was the most exciting trip of my life.

I will never forget the medical and immunization requirements for the trip. Boosters, medication, and shots for just about everything: malaria, yellow fever, cholera, tetanus, polio, measles, typhoid, hepatitis A. Prior to leaving Denver for Africa, I got so sick from one of the shots that my throat closed up and I woke in the middle of the night unable to swallow. I ended up in Emergency, wondering if I would make it to Africa. I did!

I also had some very humorous things happen before and in Africa. When I went to Emergency I thought I was dying! The doctor asked where I was going; I answered, "The Seychelles." He launched into a long, flamboyant description of the swimsuit issue of *Sports Illustrated* featuring the Seychelles! I wanted to hit him. On the way to Nairobi from New York Kennedy our plane had computer problems, necessitating an un-planned, over-night stop in Frankfurt, Germany. Our tickets had to be changed, so we could by-pass Nairobi and fly directly to the Seychelles. Our trip leader had not led a trip of this magnitude before so she was not prepared for the difficulties we experienced. We were standing in an airport waiting for a non-English speaking agent to process our plane tickets: she slowly counted them all, "One...two...three..." Then she agonizingly transferred all the tickets to her other hand and counted them all again, "One…two…three…(each ticket for the entire group)." She did this several more times before I lost patience and asked our leader, "Don't you think you should *do* something? Or we will be standing right here while our plane leaves us behind!" We had already lost a day of diving and everyone was restless. Maureen is a stunning woman, who "came-to," ran up to the counter, leaped up on it so she was leaning into the face of the agent—while we were all left staring at her "behind" draped over the counter! We also shared many good laughs among the ostriches and elephants.

After selling my business, I found many ways to keep busy. I was 41 years old. I'd had my practice for 17 years and employed 200 people. My time and energy were consumed. Suddenly I had time and energy—to do what? To learn, to grow, to stretch! Africa was just the beginning. I have been privileged to travel quite a bit and eighteen days in Africa was way too short for that trip!

Since that time I have been privileged to take a dive trip regularly with two great women friends. We have had amazing adventures in Belize, Bahamas, Cayman Islands, Turks and Caicos. I have also been diving in Saba (Netherlands Antilles), Guanaja, and Cozumel, Mexico. The joy is beyond description!

Nothing of worth exists in a vacuum. Just letting go of the old doesn't work. We must spend some time determining what to do to replace our old ways. New behaviors and thinking become comfortable by repetition. I learned to play piano when I was a child. What was the key to excellence? Practice, practice, practice. Our bodies, muscles, and brains must get accustomed to the new. For me this applies today to diving, traveling, exercising, eating in a healthy manner, writing a book, developing a whole new career.

In life, it feels as though once we reach a comfort level with a *new* behavior or way of doing/being, things change and once again we are forced to let go of the old. That's just the way life is. Life is always changing, and we are continually forced to grow and accommodate.

In a global economy with the internet and continuous high tech changes, we must deal with life changing at a faster and faster pace. Do we truly want the world to stop? Do we truly want to stop making progress? To stop changing means death. I mean to keep growing—and flowing with change. My new ways of doing/being are the best ever. I'm just getting good at it! So, I know that I will keep at it for at least one more day—today! I can manage letting go and going forward—today!

So can you. Just for one day—at a time. Just grow today. Ask yourself what do you need to let go of today? What do you need to start today? Now, do it. You can.

Opportunity is not a carrot dangling just outside your reach. You get to choose to remove restrictions and limits. Only you can.

Not anyone who loves you. Not anyone who works with you. Not your kids, wife, husband, parent, friend or lover. YOU.

Sit down right now and make a list of all the things you would like to let go. Next, make a list of all the things you would like to have in your life. Now, match them up. What will replace what and when will you be rich? When will things get easier? When will the marriage get better? When will your boss realize what you are worth? When will the kids leave home? When will your employees realize how indispensable you are? When will you have more time? *Will you change your life then?* Or will you keep repeating the patterns? If you truly want your life to be different, you will begin today. Today is where we live.

Suppose you die in a car crash tonight? Have you given all you can to your life today? Time is an important concept. Time is the same for all of us. We all have all there is: 24 hours each day. Wishing for more time is futile. The only time any of us has is NOW. We can only exist in the present moment. So, if you want to change your life, you can only change it in the present moment.

Live one day at a time
and make it a masterpiece.

PERSONAL LIST:

(Yes, just do it for yourself—there's no time like the present!)

WHAT I NEED TO LET GO OF: **WHAT I'D LIKE IN MY LIFE:**

KEY #6: EMBRACE A NEW WAY

Find JOY in your new way of being—to keep it! Remember how many times you promised yourself to diet and to do some aerobic or fitness exercises regularly? If you are like most of us, OFTEN! Perhaps you even joined a health club, thinking that a monetary investment would inspire you to work out regularly. Did it ?

The only people I know who have stayed with a fitness regime are the ones who discovered an activity or two, that they are passionate about. One friend truly enjoys running. Indeed, he needs it. He has become positively addicted! No one can decide for you what inspires you. Figure out what you enjoy, then do it. Your initial effort will then grow into a "must do" activity and lifetime commitment. Select a new behavior that is FUN! It seems to be hard for many of us to have fun—regularly, predictably, planned. It's a lot easier for us to work.

Frequently after a seminar, a client will ask me how to determine what he or she really _wants_ and enjoys in life. I ask, "What do _you_ really _love_ to do?" The client looks at me like I'm crazy! I estimate that 90% of the people I know have never asked themselves this question. We discover our joy when we stop to ask ourselves what brings us joy!

Joy is gladness, delight, exultation, rapture, satisfaction. Do you have it? Are you joyful? You deserve it. Daily! Don't wait for someone else to provide your joy. You must fill yourself. Only when you are full do have something to share. Share your joy. First, find it! What brings you joy?

What brings me joy? I absolutely love helping people with small businesses to plan and succeed, working with them to improve their teams and communications; public speaking, writing, recording; scuba diving, hiking, walking, biking, 4-wheel exploring, seeking out ghost towns; travel to faraway places, other cultures; cooking, time with friends; photography, movies, old movies on TV; reading. I love to do more things than I am probably ever going to be able to do in this lifetime!

I am learning to play with children more all the time: blowing bubbles, watching a slinky work its way down the stairs, playing jacks, being silly, having fun! Children inherently know joy . We teach them how to be serious. How sad. Such nonsense. When they grow up, they have to re-learn joy. Just like us. Let us live and teach balance.

HOW DO YOU FIGURE OUT WHAT YOU REALLY LOVE TO DO? Close yourself up in a room away from the distractions of the world. Unplug the telephones (yes!) If the doorbell rings, ignore it. Ensure no interruptions. You really can, you know! The world won't stop. Light candles or build a fire in the fireplace. Put on relaxing music. I use classical or jazz. Set the stage for your "quiet mind" to work. Gather crayons, markers, or colored pencils and a large pad of paper. Then DRAW. Ask yourself (over and over): "What do I really LOVE to do? What brings me joy?" For a full hour keep asking yourself what brings you true joy. Then *draw* it! Do no writing. Do not analyze or judge your ideas. Just brainstorm. Keep drawing.

At the end of the hour, you may analyze what you drew. Look at the patterns. Now analyze and organize the images. What do the patterns, shapes, designs, colors tell you about yourself? What feelings and memories do they stir? Have you rediscovered a hobby you can turn into an income? If you drew lots of fish—can you fish for a living? Can you buy a boat and crew? Can you open a fish market? Can you cook fish for a living?

I first did this technique after I sold my physical therapy practice. I had sold the old house and was living in a rented townhouse while my new home was being built. I had an incredible view of the foothills to the great Rocky Mountains. This focused time helped me greatly to determine how I wanted to spend the rest of my life.

IQ tests don't necessarily show our genius. My friend, Paul, is a genius. He knows it and I know it. He has one rule for life: If it isn't fun, he doesn't do it. This is true of his job, his family relationships and friendships, and tne theater. I believe he lives one of the most JOYFUL lives of anyone I know. He pays to have his clothes washed, because it isn't fun and he feels he could be doing things much more fun and creative with that time. For a living, he develops market-timing software for investment funds. Paul is more than a little successful—financially as well as personally. To him, his work is fun! Paul sees himself as a citizen of the universe. He doesn't live in one place too long. He wants to experience the whole planet to the largest extent possible. He has remodeled his life many times.

Paul came into my life when he was given a set of my audio tapes by a mutual friend. He was so impressed with "**Management by 100% Responsibility**," that he called me. We've been friends ever since.

Paul does not believe in "can't...won't...it-can't-be-done." He doesn't live in the negative and never will. Paul has generously allowed me to share with you his process for deciding *what he loves to do*, what brings him joy, and what he will do next:

SIX STEPS TO GETTING "UN-STUCK"
TO MOVING FORWARD
TO DETERMINING WHAT YOU WANT TO DO

1. First, ask yourself *the* question you need to decide now. e.g., what should you do with your career, etc.

2. *Green light sessions*: Spend 30 minutes several times over several days. NO judgment is allowed. NO "what I think I want." NO "what I *think* I can." Write as many responses to your focus question as fast as you can. (themes, bizarre, funny, serious, hard, easy, dangerous). Be creative!

3. *Priority session*: In a 30-minute session, list your priorities, roughly in order. These are your deeply-felt priorities—not what you believe you *should* do, think and feel. Ask yourself, "What are my 3-6 most important life priorities?

4. *Highlight session*: In a 30-minute session, highlight, star, circle, or underline which priorities feel like what you *want* to do. (Right now, not concerned with *how*.)

5. *Visualization sessions*: Visualize one role per day. Actually imagine yourself *in* each potential role/position/activity. How do you feel? What does the role look like? Where are you in the image? What are you doing? *Be* in the picture. (Still not concerned with *how*.)

6. *Another visualization*: Envision actually attracting all the circumstances or situations that will make your focused desire happen. *Now* you begin to explore how.

CONCLUSION: After this process, you are much more prepared and able to make the decisions necessary to go out and create your new future!

> *If you don't have what you want,*
> *you are not committed to it 100%.*
> *Dr. Robert Anthony*

I don't believe there are truly any victims on the planet. People do grow up being victimized. People do grow up without privileges and comfort. People do live in poverty and live where there is war, disease, oppression, and no food. Many people do live in horrible conditions. But you know what? Some of those people leave their circumstances. They are not victims. They are "choosers."

People choose to be victimized; they play victim to their pasts and to their circumstances. It doesn't have to be that way. Generally, people do not *consciously* or intentionally choose their unhappy lives; certainly children don't. Positive changes in our lives are conscious decisions not to play victim. We must take conscious action to change our lives for the better by making non-victim decisions.

How do mentally and spiritually healthy individuals handle their abusive pasts or victimizations?
- They stop denial.
- They acknowledge the reality of their situations.
- They *feel* the feelings.
- They *deal*, then they *heal*.
- They forgive the perpetrator(s).

You don't have to remain in a position where anyone is hurting you NOW. If you truly are or were underprivileged, abused, used, victimized, YOU CAN CHANGE TODAY. Continued obsession about your past mistreatments is victimizing yourself, giving the victimizer continued power over you. You cannot change the past. You cannot do enough guilt to pay for past wrongs or undo them. YOU CAN LEARN FROM THE PAST AND CHOOSE NOT TO REPEAT IT. *No on is continuing the victimization today but you.* No matter how much you blame your parents, spouse, teacher, the marines, the war, or whatever is your particular scapegoat, get help if you need it. Deal with it. Otherwise, you are victimizing yourself.

How you live in this present moment is a choice. Guilt will not help. It cannot and does not change anything. Guilt only makes you feel worse. In my "**Management by 100% Responsibility**" seminar, I draw the following graphic to demonstrate past, present and future:

```
           PAST                PRESENT              FUTURE
BODY:_____→X_____
            
MIND:  X◄_____
```

        Usual here:
        ~~GUILT~~
        Better to:
        LEARN.

Your body is firmly planted in the present, attending the seminar. I can see, smell, touch, feel to prove that your *body* is here in the present. Your *mind*, however, can go anywhere it wants and may very well go back to yesterday, last year, even many years ago. The elderly often go back many years mentally to pleasant memories when the spouse was alive and the body was free of pain. Certainly, memories are great; in fact, crucial to mental health. However, as Louise Hay says in *You Can Heal Your Life,* **the point of power is always in the present moment.** Only in *this* moment do we truly live.

You may be bodily present at a seminar but thinking about yesterday's happenings, or what happened ten years ago, or what your spouse said this morning at breakfast.. You may feel guilt over real or imagined harms. I ask seminar participants if they have ever been able to "do" enough guilt to change their past actions and poor choices. They smile, admitting they have not. Certainly, we can't change what was done to us. But the question comes, "What should you do with your past? Should you just ignore it?" No. But neither should you feel guilty. From today forward you can use what you *learned* from your past to create positive change.

Guilt is a choice. If you did harm to someone, clean-up the past by apologizing. Making amends. Paying back. In some significant way take responsibility for causing another pain.

THIS IS YOU DOING
GUILT.
CHOOSE NOT TO!

Webster's Dictionary defines guilt as blame, fault, culpability. Condemnation often involves shame, too.

To proceed, get clear on your feelings and thoughts. Have you ever thought about feelings and thoughts? *Webster* defines feelings as *sensation, an emotion.* Can someone else make you feel anything? No. Your feelings are uniquely your own based upon your beliefs, experiences and values. Your feelings can only come from your thoughts.

Where do thoughts come from? Can anyone outside you make you think certain thoughts? No. During a seminar of 50 participants, each person hears the same words different. Therefore, we can say that guilt is totally a choice. Guilt is a feeling based on chosen thoughts. You can change your thoughts and, thus, your feelings. No one else can do that for you. You alone have that power.

There is no real truth. You may happen to agree with me based upon your own set of beliefs, experiences, and values. Therefore, all 50 seminar participants hear exactly what they came to hear.

If you were hurt by someone, your only options for joy are: Feel the pain. Deal with it. Let yourself heal. To be free to move on, you also must forgive. How do you forgive? When your anger is justified and you want to hold it and cherish it forever, how do you forgive someone else's hurtful action toward you?

Start with *willingness* to forgive.

I agree with Louise Hay when she tells us: "Choose to release the past and forgive everyone, yourself included. You may not know how to forgive. You may not want to forgive. However, being willing to forgive starts your healing process." Here is an affirmation to set you free:

I forgive myself for not being the person I want to be.
I forgive others, and set myself free.

Create your own affirmation for forgiveness to begin healing.

Forgiveness frees you to learn from your past. When you have learned your life lessons, you stop playing victim and you do not repeat your past patterns.

What about the future? With your body in the present, your mind in the future is doing what? Frequently, *worrying*. My dear little grandmother worries about me flying so much and traveling alone. She means, "I love you very much and have great concern

55

for your safety." I tell her, "If you're going to worry, don't pray. If you're going to pray, don't worry." Can she worry enough to keep me from dying in a plane crash? Can I worry sufficiently to prevent a natural disaster or the death of a loved one? Worry looks like this:

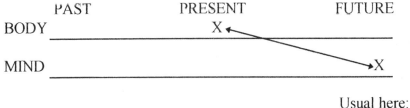

PAST	PRESENT	FUTURE

BODY _____ X _____

MIND _____ X

Usual here:
~~WORRY~~

Better to:
PLAN

Worry is like guilt—totally unproductive. Worry doesn't change anything. Worry cannot alter the future, any more than guilt can alter the past. So like the song says, "Don't Worry, Be Happy!" Being happy really is a choice, as is worry a choice.

Clearly, then, instead of worry use your past experiences. Use what you learn from your past to PLAN your future. We are not able to control all factors, but when we utilize our experiences, including our mistakes, we give up blame and shame and we plan ahead—to the best of our ability.

PLANNING WORKS WHEN YOU DO THE GROUNDWORK AND LEAVE THE RESULTS TO THE DIVINE, or whatever Source you believe in.

As a seminar participant, you may worry about the future or just ahead to tonight: Did I remember to take the fish out of the refrigerator? What movie will we watch? Will my spouse remember to pick up the kids? What about the ball game? Can we pay the rent tomorrow? It isn't significant how far your mind goes into the future, except that when your mind wanders, you leave the present. And the present is the only time-frame you can change and in which you literally live. Living in the present moment is where all the power for change is.

	PAST	PRESENT	FUTURE
Body		X	
Mind		X	

There are risks in the present. When you truly live here, you have to address what is real *right now*. Life is scary here and can be very uncomfortable. You are vulnerable in the present. It is in the present that you quit blaming your spouse for all his or her shortcomings. When s/he asks: "What is the problem right *now?*" you must not address the last ten years, (archeological problem solving) but literally right *now*. It takes discipline to keep your thoughts in the present. But, the present is also where all good experiences happen:

- great art
- good music
- true intimacy
- rich friendships
- spiritual experiences
- nature experiences

- good feelings
- all feelings
- love
- creativity.

One of my first incredibly powerful realizations of "present moment" living came after my father was seriously burned. (Dad and Mom love to snorkel, but they don't scuba dive.) Shortly after the occurrence of Dad's burns, I went to Cozumel, Mexico to be certified for open water (out-of-swimming-pool) diving. I had just mastered neutral buoyancy, a state wherein I didn't float to the surface nor sink in the sand; I just floated perfectly level, not touching anything. Soon after certification, I was diving close to the ocean floor. The water was clear azure blue, like a Colorado sky in the autumn. Visibility was about 150 feet! The sand was white like pure sugar. All colors were intensified and my senses were greatly heightened. I looked up toward the sky through the water. Long, sparkling, gold streams of sunlight shot through the water. A large school of Angel fish swam by, in perfect precision, right through the golden light fall. The vision was powerful! I was physically and emotionally struck by the beauty. "This is the only moment I have," I realized with shock. I remember thinking "I must memorize every detail so I can re-create it for Dad and take it back to him!" I was in the present moment. It was the only place I could be—in that time—both physically and mentally.

The most powerful lesson for me in that "present moment" was the realization that nothing even five minutes past had any real significance. In that sense, the past did not exist. I was captivated by the singular moment. What would happen next would also enthrall me—then.

Floating in the sea, in this moment was my reality. It was *all*. I could not think ahead to what would happen when I returned to the boat above, or when I returned home. I *knew* that in those moments I would be fully *there*. I would be fully present wherever I was. My life then became vivid and real!

Another exquisite "present moment" came when one summer I has hiking to the top of a mystical, magical mountain close to Aspen, Mt. Sopris. Twin summits rise to 13,000 feet. My long-legged companion, Don, was climbing over huge, sharp boulders with great ease; unlike the way I enthusiastically squirreled over those boulders with my short legs—four times his steps and strides. I must have been an Indian who lived on that mountain in another life. When I go to Glenwood Springs, I always spend some time looking at and meditating upon Mt. Sopris, watching the sunsets turn the great monolith bright pink.

As my friend and I hiked up the mountain, a summer thunderstorm became threatening; numerous hikers ahead of us were turning around. I had no intention of turning back—short of a life-threatening situation; we had backpacked in to camp at Dinkle lake at the base of the peaks. We watched the storm come down the valley from McClure Pass, past Redstone to Glenwood, then turn around the mountain and head up toward Aspen. It was awesome!

When we reached the second summit, we looked down on the town of Redstone. Crimson-colored stone cascaded all the way down the mountain. The grass was as green and soft as any putting green. The sky was cobalt. Huge, fluffy, white post-storm clouds spread across the horizon. My heart stopped still! "This is perfect!" I declared into the vast open space. "This is as good as I ever need for life to be!" The moment was exultant. I was totally in the present moment. The all-encompassing sensation was mental, physical, spiritual, and emotional. Full value! This was real intimacy with life. Full joy. This moment was worth all the discipline and awareness it took me to make the decision to *Be here now!*

Another "present moment" experience was at a Yanni concert with a young friend, Barb, just graduating from college. She was newly sober and had never been to a concert sober. The concert was at Red Rocks Park in the mountains just west of Denver—a stunning location for a concert. We sat in fresh air, out-of-doors, surrounded by giant red rocks. The setting sun turned the rocks a glowing crimson. Yanni's piano concertos lifted us. My miracle "moment" was watching my young friend's face as she truly *experienced* the music. We both were totally *there*.

I have a new friend in my life. Recently, we went hiking to photograph mountain goats. Bob asked me, "Can you really stay in the present moment all the time?" I answered, "No." However, I can choose to be *present* in the high country of Webster Pass where the weather changes instantly and sleet blows so fast it seems the earth is whirling underneath the clouds. Yes, sir. You betcha!

Living in the present moment takes discipline and desire. We can only embrace a new way in *this* moment. We cannot find joy in any moment but the one we are in. We stop playing victim and leave the past behind—in the present moment.

Once we have gained the ability to live in the present moment, we are prepared to offer this gift to others. We are ready to serve others. We are assured of continued high quality present moments by surrounding ourselves with positive, supportive people who share our dreams with us.

> *There is no denying that most of us, when we*
> *arrive at a place, immediately begin to think*
> *of other places to which we may go from it.*
> Mercelene Cox

EPILOGUE: SERVE OTHERS

What good is "self-improvement," "self-help," "changing self" if it is only self-serving? A friend, Jerry, whom I very much admire, said something the other day which I take to heart. He noted that the problem with self-help books and many motivational speakers is that they are all about SELF: What can I get for ME? What will this do for ME? How can I improve MY life, finances, relationships, et al? "They are too self-centered," Jerry said. "Without a willingness to share the good, and spend time, energy and resources in service to others, isn't it all meaningless? Isn't it all just so much empty talk?" Good sense, my friend.

Every great religion, philosophy, theory, belief system, and spiritual teacher I have studied has, in some way emphasized service. Commonalities in these beliefs are the basic principles of love, honesty, integrity, acceptance, faith, trust, courage, humility, forgiveness, surrender, willingness, freedom, perseverance, patience, *and service.*

If we don't commit to service, we find ourselves locked into dark and dangerous places. When we reach out and find service that suits us and our personalities, we find our unique place and abilities in society.

I have sought my niche over many years and have found it in legion hours of volunteered time to people recovering from addictions: phone time, personal time, meals prepared, overnights provided. I am privileged to see miracles happen: people getting productive, love-filled lives back.

My friend, Cia, spends time at a public broadcasting station seeking financial support for quality television. She also rides in the "Courage Classic," a 150-mile bicycle ride to collect pledges for Children's Hospital. She does not have to do this. She could just donate. She enjoys giving her time and personal commitments to the causes in which she believes.

Another friend, Deborah, spends five hours a week helping at a "half-way house" for women coming out of prison; they are still serving time. Most of them have three felonies or more. Some of them are drug addicts, some alcoholics, some drug dealers, and others have committed crimes of various types for which they are learning to take responsibility. Deb's motivation flows from deep gratitude that her own addictions led her close to prison herself. Only by grace and sobriety was she spared. The service work gratifies her because she gets to be a part of people's learning new life skills in a practical and responsible manner. I knew Deb for over a year before she told me she gives this service.

Some of my family members have gone to Africa, Tibet, and China as missionaries. My parents, more than ten years after leaving Ruanda, still send money to support children in the schools there and to help feed the little ones caught up in the political chaos.

Many of my friends don't tell what they do to be of service because telling might be for self-glorification. Humility and private sharing are more of value to them.

There are many ways we can make a difference in people's lives. We can serve in professional capacities as well as personal and spiritual. I know that I am meant to serve. I give to the power of good on the planet through speaking, training, books, audio tapes, consulting, volunteering, serving on a Board of Directors— *anything else that shows up! Beauty, hope and love are to be shared!*

Surround yourself with positive, Supportive people who share your dreams!

Choose whom you surround yourself with—at work, home, play. Otherwise, you might not have the encouragement you need from others during your tough times. (You may have less control over this at work. Do the best you can. You can choose your work friends.)

Be prepared. There will be tough times. You already know this. You have tried to change patterns or behaviors before. Even when our intentions are great, lasting change can be challenging at times. We need others.

Where do you find supportive people who will help you keep and share your dreams? Maybe they are already in your life? If the people in your family or home do not seem to be on your side or willing to support you, perhaps they do not know you want or need their support!

Be clear with your loved ones and friends about what you need and how you need for them to help you. Support means *aid, uphold, endure, maintain*. Then you ask for what you need. Clearly. Plainly. Directly. This is no time for manipulation or games, such as "He knows I need to be told he loves me, or that I am beautiful, or that he cares or is there for me, or that he wants me to do well..."

Generally, I am straightforward and direct. However, in truly intimate conversations or when I need personal support, I continue to work very hard to be: Clear. Plain. Direct. And to just ASK. It works.

If you have not found positive, supportive people in your life, then actively and with clear purpose seek them out. There is much negativity in our world. It takes effort and active, conscious choosing to find and only associate with positive people. Look for these people in churches, groups, meetings, at work, in support groups and clubs where people share your interests. *Think way outside your box!*

Remember my friend Paul and his winning formula for changing directions and discovering what you love to do? Here is Paul's story about how he learned to live his life fully and positively; how he discovered the power of surrounding himself with positive, supportive people who share his dreams:

In terms of preparing for a promising career, Paul began life on the wrong foot. Neither of his parents completed high school. His own schooling began in a very low-income ghetto neighborhood. His educational experience was not particularly stimulating. Then he mistook boredom and poor grades for an inability to learn. He dropped out of high school, though eventually he obtained a diploma through an alternative, trade-oriented public school. Paul began his career poorly-educated and essentially illiterate.

After several years of disappointing dead-end jobs, a brief tour of military duty, and a divorce, Paul was a single parent. He had come to accept his lot in life—an unrewarding career with a limited financial potential. It was pretty clear to him that he was on a course for continued disappointment in life.

Fortunately, however, Paul met a person who shared some motivational concepts with him and encouraged him to read some short articles and listen to audio tapes by authors like Maxwell Maltz, W. Clement Stone, and Earl Nightingale. Though these new ideas were inspiring to Paul, it was difficult for him to believe they would work for him. After all, he had a very poor education and limited job skills. Nonetheless, as time went on, Paul came to a point when he said to himself, "What have I got to lose? Maybe, just maybe, I could learn to *choose differently* for my future. Maybe I am *playing victim*, letting my past be an excuse for not going anywhere in the present."

The thought of a new life and a bright future was intriguing and compelling to Paul, but he was still guarded since he had never experienced success. So he decided to put these new motivational concepts to the test. He enrolled in a night class at the local junior college. However, instead of just taking the class, he threw himself into it. After all, if he just muddled through, that would prove nothing and the class would be a complete waste of his time. Paul decided not to focus on the exam scores or the final grade. Rather he decided to make the experience as fun and exciting as possible. He could not imagine being able to persist in this class if it were as painful and unrewarding as in high school. The *test* would, once and for all, prove or disprove the merit of all these hypothetical motivational concepts he'd been reading about. If the concepts proved to be false, then Paul would go on with his life as usual. A few weeks of his spare time were all that he would lose.

At first, the course work seemed impossible. All the other students seemed much smarter and better prepared. The homework was difficult. The first exam scores were disappointing. At times Paul felt like giving up. But he decided to see this *test* through to the end. So, night after night he persisted. He attended every class, handed in every homework assignment, read all the materials and studied for every exam. Frequently Paul stayed after class to talk with the instructor and ask questions.

As the weeks wore on, the material slowly began to make sense. Paul was able to contribute to class discussions and actually did well on the midterm exam. One success led to another and in the end, he received the highest score in the class on the final exam and an A for the course. More importantly, Paul discovered that his former self-image as a victim of his past experiences and the belief that he was doomed to repeat those experiences was absolutely false. He could indeed learn and it was very rewarding.

By the time Paul had finished this class, he had become "addicted" to motivational books and audio tapes! He continued to learn and apply what he learned. He began trying to imagine his future possibilities. What would he do with his newfound knowledge? Soon, an old dream started coming back to him, an "impossible" dream that he'd had many years before. As I child frequently Paul pretended he was a great engineer or scientist, but that dream had died, as he became more and more discouraged with life in general and school in particular. But now maybe, just maybe, his dream was possible. Did he dare to believe that he could make it through college? The thought both excited and frightened him.

At this point Paul was about to learn the most valuable lesson of his life. In attempting to follow his dream he felt very vulnerable. He was a prime target for every nay-sayer in the universe. They seemed to crawl out of the woodwork and enjoy giving him the "benefit" of all their great wisdom!

The nay-sayers were well meaning They probably did not consciously know the damage they did. They thought they were giving Paul some great advice "for his own good." The most devastating nay-sayers were his family members, trusted friends, and those in-places-of-authority-and-thus-know-these-things-and-to-question-their-opinion-was-heresy.

The nay-sayers told Paul all the reasons why he could not possibly accomplish his goal. They pointed out how naïve he was to even consider such an undertaking. "Do you know what you are getting yourself into?" they asked. "I've seen people try that one before, and they fell right on their faces!" They went on to point out every little "fact" that supported their assessments. "You are too old/young/fat/skinny. You don't have the right looks/personality/aptitude/background/training/credentials. You're not the right gender/race." And on and on. Worse yet, the nay-sayer's "facts" were very often true.

67

When Paul announced that he was going to go to engineering school, his boss said, "After all we've done for you here at the company, and this is how you repay us? Hey, this is a company on the move. If you leave now, you'll regret it. We'll have to replace you and there is no way you can get your old job back. This is the biggest mistake of your entire life."

Of course his most helpful friend said, "There is no way that a single parent can afford child-care without a full-time job. You are being selfish. You've got to think of your daughter." Another friend just laughed and said "You, go to college? Yeah, right!"

The most devastating nay-sayer was the Admissions Counselor at the university who pointed out several "facts" that were hard to deny. "Paul, I've got to tell it to you straight. We turn away thousands of applicants who have B-averages, and you graduated in the bottom ten percent of your class. My hands are tied. I simply cannot approve your application, then deny someone else who has a much better scholastic record. Let's be realistic. The students who get into our engineering school are at the top of their classes. They've been through all the college prep classes, calculus, physics, and chemistry. You haven't even had trigonometry, let alone science classes. Other than the one junior college class, you haven't had any formal education for quite some time. Our freshman engineering students have been preparing for years for engineering school; even then, twenty five percent of them won't make it through their freshman year. With your background, how can you possibly keep up? Then there is the problem of your financial aid. You've saved enough for the first semester's tuition and books; but neither you nor your parents have the necessary financial capability beyond that. With your high school record, institutional financial aid is simply out of the question. I am sorry to be so direct, but it would be unfair of me to get your hopes up."

Paul made one last desperate attempt by asking, "Isn't there some way I could get into this university, even on a part-time basis?" The counselor replied, "Absolutely not. Not as a student anyway. Paul, let me be blunt. The only way you could get into this university would be to apply for a janitor's position!"

And so Paul's dream died. The counselor's "facts" were irrefutable. Perhaps his boss and friends had been right also. At this point Paul began to wonder how he could have been so naïve? He hit a brick wall. Obviously he could not go forward. Then again, he soon found he could not simply go back to his old life style either—living one day to the next, with no hope of a brighter future. He had hit bottom. He was angry, depressed and miserable.

In desperation, finally Paul decided to put the motivational concepts to the test once again. "Persistence and creativity" the motivational tapes said. "If you can't get through the front door, try the back." Paul decided to plead his case before the Dean of the Engineering School. Instantly he ran into the next nay-sayer—the Dean's secretary. She, too, had all the right "facts." "The Dean is a very busy person with absolutely no spare time. He simply doesn't see any applicants until they have been accepted by admissions."

However, after several pleading calls, to Paul's surprise the secretary said the Dean would be having lunch in his office that day and if Paul were extremely brief, the dean would listen. In the meeting, the Dean quietly ate his lunch while Paul gushed out his story non-stop from beginning to end. Paul even told the dean all about the "facts" the Admissions Counselor had told him. Finally, Paul admitted that all the facts everyone had brought to his attention were true; what's more, he didn't know if he could make it through engineering school. However, if there were any exceptions to the rules, he wanted a chance to try, if for no other reason than to prove it to himself.

The Dean let Paul finish his story, then picked up the phone, called the Admissions Counselor and requested that Paul be given a "special student" status. This meant that all Paul's courses would be taken on a "no-credit" basis and he could only enroll in a class if there was space left after everyone else had enrolled. The Dean told Paul his biggest hurdle would be freshman calculus and suggested two remedial math classes to give him the background he needed. He also told Paul that if he maintained a good grade-point average, he could petition the College of Engineering Council to see if they would retroactively accept his past credits and allow him to enroll in a degree program. The Dean warned Paul, "There are no promises, Paul. The Council could deny your petition."

All Paul could say was "Great. Fine. That's OK! All I want is a chance." As Paul left the Dean's office, the Dean winked at him and smiled, saying, "Oh, by the way. I chair the College of Engineering Council, and I'll be expecting that petition. Don't let me down!" As Paul left, he didn't remember his feet even touching the floor!

Paul graduated from engineering school, third in his class, with "Special Honors." Getting this degree was by no means easy. In fact it was even tougher than he had imagined. But it was also the most exciting and thrilling adventure of his entire life. He was elected president of two engineering honorary societies and he started a tutorial program in which top students volunteered their time to help students who were struggling during their freshman years. Upon graduation, Paul received 13 job offers. The company he joined put him through graduate school at Stanford University, all expenses paid. During his career Paul has founded three high-tech companies, lectured at three universities, and become a millionaire before he was 40.

How did Paul overcome these irrefutable "facts" that his friends and the Admissions Counselor had so generously brought to his attention? He declares that the nay-sayers did not realize that a dream coupled with a burning desire transcends seemingly impenetrable obstacles. Paul created circumstances that would bring his dream into reality. He did not buy into the nay-sayer's arguments—and his dream lived!

I am privileged to know *many* magnificent, unselfish, spiritually growing human beings. They live the seven keys. They choose to change their lives. After hurting enough, they all asked for help and accepted responsibility for their choices. The did not quit. They grabbed onto the new and let go of the old. They no longer play victims. Today, they fully embrace finding joy and bringing joy to others. As a result of putting the 7 Keys into their lives, they are able to serve others. These growing, loving human beings surround themselves with positive, supportive people who share their dreams.

Discovering and fulfilling your dreams, creating positive change in your life, is a life's journey. There is no quick fix. Each new concept, experience, understanding builds upon and reinforces those that came before. I have come to know that the journey is much more important than the destination! I will choose to continue growing and seeking while I:

Cherish Yesterday,
Dream Tomorrow,
Live Today.

Selected Bibliography

Anthony, R. *Think*. New York: Berkley Books, 1985.

Canfield, J., and Hansen, M *Chicken Soup for the Soul*. Deerfield Beach, FL: Health Communications, Inc., 1993.

Hay, L. *You Can Heal Your Life*. Santa Monica, CA: Hay House, 1987.

Huston, T., and Rizzo, K. *More Than Mountains: The Todd Huston Story*. Boise, ID: Pacific Press Publishing Association, 1995.

Wholey, D. *The Courage to Change*. Boston, MA: Houghton Mifflin Company, 1984.

Willey, T. *The Power of Choice*. Denver, CO: Berwick House, 1988.

READER SURVEY:

Open Mind Publishing would greatly appreciate you taking *two minutes* to complete this reader survey so that we may continue to meet the needs of the reading public:

Please print:
NAME:_____
ADDRESS:_____
　　　　　City:_____State:____Zip:_____
TELEPHONE NUMBER:_____

Did you enjoy the *7 Keys*?　(please check one) ___yes___no
Would you purchase another book by this author? ___yes___no
Do you frequently purchase self help/inspirational books?
　　　　　　　　　　　　　　　　　　　　___yes___no
Do you frequently purchase inspirational audio tapes?
　　　　　　　　　　　　　　　　　　　　___yes___no
Do you frequently purchase educational audio tapes?
　　　　　　　　　　　　　　　　　　　　___yes___no
Do you frequently purchase business audio tapes?___yes___no
Do you prefer video tapes to audio tapes?　　___yes___no
What made you decide to purchase *7 Keys*?
　　___price　___topic　___knew author　___seminar

Additional comments you would like to make to help us serve you better:_____
_____
_____

Thank you very much for taking the time to respond to this survey. Please return survey to: Open Mind Publishing, 23 S. Indiana Pl. Golden, CO 80401. As a special thank you we will send you a valuable Gift Certificate.

It is our pleasure to serve you!

DESCRIPTIONS OF OTHER AVAILABLE PRODUCTS:

Linda McNeil is a public speaker, team builder and consultant who has recorded a number of seminar materials on audio tapes with accompanying textbooks. They are available specific to physical therapy (PT) or other businesses. Please order accordingly. Descriptions of the products follow:

Management by 100% Responsibility—Three powerful 60 minute audio tapes and workbooks dealing with attitudes in the workplace. Featuring real world examples, this is an excellent introduction to management's roles and requirements. Demonstrates how different personalities communicate and tend to deal with stress and change. Incl. handouts and textbook. (appropriate for all) $49.95

Dynamite Customer Service—Two entertaining 45 minute audio tapes with textbook that review what it takes to really connect with your customers. Customers will not just be satisfied, but delighted. Includes information for improving front office procedures and telephone etiquette. Incl. textbook. (PT and small business) $29.95

Future Planning—Two 40 minute audio tapes with workbook, usable forms and computer diskette for ongoing duplication of forms. This package is designed to lead you through the process of business planning and marketing strategy in a one day do-it-yourself format. 10 keys for truly successful planning. (PT and small business) $49.95

What Does My Staff REALLY Want?--One 40 minute audio tape with handout. If you want to better understand staff motivation, this is the tape for you. The ideas were obtained from staff and client interviews over years of employing hundreds of people, followed by ten years of consulting. (PT) $14.95

7 Keys to Changing Any Attitude or Circumstance in Your Life-
77 page book for only $7.77 which will change your life—if you are ready to change any attitude or circumstance in your life. Be inspired and enjoy Lin McNeil's personal and professional change experiences!

ORDER FORM NEXT PAGE:

ORDER FORM:

Name/Title_____

Company_____

Address_____

City_____State_____Zip_____

Phone_____

SPECIAL OFFER:
10% OFF when you order at least three products
and only one shipping/handling charge of $5.00

Satisfaction Guaranteed or your money back.

NAME OF PRODUCT:	PRICE:	NO.:	S/H:	$ TOTAL:
Management by 100% R.. (all)	$49.95		$3.00	$
Future Planning (for PT)	$49.95		$3.00	$
Future Planning (Sm.Bus.)	$49.95		$3.00	$
Dynamite Customer (for PT)	$29.95		$3.00	$
Dynamite Customer (Sm.Bus.)	$29.95		$3.00	$
What Does My Staff... (for PT)	$14.95		$3.00	$
BOOK: 7 Keys to...(all)	$7.77		$3.00	$
TOTALS:				

Mail Check Payable to:
Choices & Changes Unlimited
23 S. Indiana Pl.
Golden, CO 80401
or charge to:
Visa_____ MasterCard_____
Card Number:_____
Exp. Date:_____/_____

OR CALL TO CHARGE:
(303) 277-9488 / 1-800-748-3488

TRAINING AND DEVELOPMENT SEMINARS

by Linda McNeil

The following seminars are available for your staff, association, convention or public event:

Management by 100% Responsibility—a full day course which examines attitudes on the job. Practical tools are presented which include team building—dealing with conflict and change, improving communication skills, spending more time mentally "at-home" while at work, clarifying job parameters between employer and employees, productivity, and eliminating excuses from daily work and personal behavior.

Dynamite Customer Service—Four to six hour course focuses on the importance of providing excellent customer support. Information for new programs and enhancing current ones is provided in an entertaining and positive way. Tools are given for dealing with the public, telephone etiquette, and communicating with angry and/or difficult clients.

Future Planning—Four to six hour course complete with actual consulting forms for doing your own business strategy and marketing plan in one day. Analyzes business strengths, weaknesses, target markets, and provides ten keys to planning success.

How to Build Teams and Relationships—Four to eight hour course which enhances work relationships and communications by utilizing self-administered, self-interpreted DiSC^{tm} personality profiles, with many interactive exercises. Fun and educational!

7 Keys to Changing Any Attitude or Circumstance in Your Life-Utilizes Linda McNeil's book published 10/97 for a full day of interaction, fun, enlightenment and inspiration. If you are ready to change, this course will give you exactly what you need—now!

Choices & Changes Unlimited   Call: (303) 277-9488
23 S. Indiana Pl. Golden, CO   or 1-800-748-3488

DiSC^{tm} and Other Personality Profiles
Learning to Work Together
by Linda L. McNeil, TeamBuilder/Consultant/Speaker

The *DiSC Personal Profile System*^{tm} helps each person learn about his or her own strengths, weaknesses and tendencies under pressure or stress. Understanding ourselves and others helps us to:

- Understand our effect on others
- Appreciate each other's differences
- Adapt strategies to communicate better
- Listen more effectively
- Build better relationships
- Enhance conflict resolution skills
- Improve staff retention
- Improve hiring practices and protocol

DiSC^{tm} is one of the most successful and widely-used personal and professional development tools ever created. A self-reporting personality profile from the Carlson Learning Company in Minneapolis, MN since 1972, Linda McNeil prefers it to other profiles because of its simplicity and practical applicability.

The four primary descriptive personality types include:

- *Dominance*
- *Influence*
- *Steadiness*
- *Conscientiousness*

While everyone has every trait, some traits are stronger in each individual. These characteristics determine our behavior as we work and play with others. There is no "right" or "best" characteristic, so there is no need to judge, label, or limit behaviors.

DiSC^{tm} can be administered to individuals or groups by Linda McNeil, who is trained and certified. Linda can also train someone in your company to administer the profile to employees.

*Call Choices & Changes Unlimited: (303) 277-9488 / 1-800-748-3488